Make It Count

Five Strategies You Can Count On
To Get The Most Out Of Life

Preston Cave

MinistryCue

Copyright © 2019 by Preston Cave
Ministry Cue Publishing
500 West Bluebonnet Dr. Granbury, TX 76048

www.ministrycue.com

Cover Design and Chapter Graphics: Brandon Cave

www.hellohealey.com

Unless otherwise stated, all Scripture references are taken from the Holy Bible, New International Version NIV Copyright © 1973, 1978, 1984 by International Bible Society. Used by permission of *HYPERLINK* "http://www.zondervan.com/" Zondervan. All rights reserved.

All rights reserved. No part of this book may be reproduced, scanned, or distributed in any printed or electronic form without written permission.
First Edition: January 2019
Printed in the United States of America
ISBN: 9781798720653

To the many Lakeside members who are helping broken people become whole and whole people become broken for broken people.

Contents

Foreword

Strategy #1 – *One Purpose*   1

Strategy #2 – *Two Rules*   10

Strategy #3 – *Three Decisions*   20

Strategy #4 – *Two Priorities*   34

Strategy #5 – *One Person*   50

Conclusion   70

FOREWORD

Two words exist today that most people will agree are important, yet they will seldom implement. These two words are *discipline* and *strategy*. As a professional athlete I understand the importance of living a life of discipline and strategy. It has been said that you can make progress or you can make excuses, but you can't make both. *Discipline* and *strategy* are the defining factors between becoming a person of excuses or a person of progress. What we choose to do with these two words will affect the trajectory of our future. Preston has done a great job helping us learn this principle. He has always been a strategic thinker, so I am not at all surprised he decided to call each section of this booklet a "strategy" instead of a "chapter".

He and I became friends several years ago when I followed him as the student pastor of a church he had previously served. It didn't take long for me to recognize that he truly loved the Bride of Christ. I could see it in the way he interacted with me, as well as others in the trenches of ministry. I never felt like anything but a close friend to him from the beginning.

The sign of a great leader is not what *they* can accomplish, but what *those that follow them* are able to accomplish. I quickly saw the fruits of his labor in the church he previously served. I found that the work he had completed made it easy for me to hit the ground running and be able to help the students go to the next level in their relationship with Jesus. Preston did the dirt work so there would be a healthy infrastructure in place for future leaders.

One of the best ways to develop a healthy infrastructure in any ministry is to help those in the church live a life of *discipline* and *strategy*. This booklet is an attempt to help new believers learn five basic strategies to grow closer to Jesus. It is also a great reminder for seasoned believers to stay focused on what matters most in life. If every believer in Jesus would discipline himself or herself to live out these five strategies I believe the church would be healthy and thriving, and the world would be a better place.

As an Evangelist and President of a non-profit ministry I am always looking for discipleship tools. This booklet is a wonderful summary of the basics of Christianity and can help us all understand what it means to be a true follower of Jesus. I will be using it with new believers for years to come.

Jared Greer
American Ninja Warrior
President of Overcoming Obstacles
www.obstacleministry.com

Strategy in a Quote

"Help broken people become whole and whole people become broken for broken people."

2 Strategy 1 – One Purpose

There once was a man who was hired to build a wall. His employer showed him the place where the wall was to be constructed, then said, "I'll be back at lunch to give you further instructions."

The man was so excited about his new job and began to speculate as to the purpose of the wall. He wondered what would become of the wall. Would it be a luxurious skyscraper? Maybe it would be for a secret government building that would contain all the secrets of the world. Or maybe it would be more serious than that. Maybe it would become the headquarters of a medical center in charge of finding the cure for every disease known to man.

No matter how majestic or significant the purpose, he would be known as the one that built the wall. He felt a sense of pride as he positioned each brick, knowing that this was such an important project and he was helping to leave his mark on history.

Lunch came quickly. His employer returned to marvel at his wonderful creation. The boss said, "Great job building this wall! Now I want you to begin to dismantle it until closing time."

The man was extremely confused. What about the luxurious hotel? What about the cure for cancer? What about the building? All the visions of what this wall might become had just been dismantled in a single moment.

The next day was no different. Morning to noon was spent building a wall, only to be followed by dismantling it before closing time. This lasted for an entire week. The man felt like his life was a waste, and after only one week the man resigned from his job and decided that building a wall was not what he was called to do.

Obviously, this is just a modern day parable. But what is the point of this story? *Purpose* matters. A life without purpose is like building a wall just to tear it down again. It wastes time. It wastes energy. It wastes resources. And the worst part about it is that we never actually accomplish anything. There is something to be said about having a purpose in life. Everybody wants to be remembered for something. People want to feel as though their life matters, like they are making a difference for the greater good. People want to outlive their life. But how do we do this? One word: Legacy.

Legacy is when we do something so significant that it actually affects the generations that follow. Legacy never happens by accident. It is the result of intentional living. It happens when we live a life of selflessness, when we focus on others more than ourselves. The only way to affect the generations after us is to live forward, to live with eyes toward the future. We should live *in* the future. This should encourage us to start with the future in view and work our way backwards. We should train ourselves to see the *future* potential of every person, including ourselves, *now*.

One of the main reasons Jesus came to this earth was to restore the broken relationship that humans had with God. He was looking into the future and he saw, not what *is*, but what *could be*. Jesus knew that sin had broken God's perfect creation and he wanted to help broken people become whole. How would he do this? By becoming broken himself. He would sacrifice his life on a Roman cross and rise from the dead on the third day, according to the scriptures.[1] Fifty days after his resurrection he would pour out his Holy Spirit on one hundred and twenty people in an upper room and pretty much give them the same purpose: Help broken people become whole. Jesus knew that when a broken person became whole they would be so grateful and delighted that they would want to help other broken people become whole. So the cycle began in the first century and has continued until this day. The cycle is this: Help broken people become whole and whole people become broken for broken people.

Strategy in a Quote

"Help broken people become whole, and whole people become broken for broken people."

---

[1] 1 Corinthians 15:3-4

Strategy 1 – One Purpose

This was Jesus' original purpose, and this still is our purpose today. It is the picture of rebuilding a broken wall that someone left unfinished and making it into a beautiful, majestic building. It is a life worth living and a path towards leaving a legacy. Think about the innumerable amount of people that could be transformed if only Christians, as whole people, would become broken for broken people. What better purpose is there to live for than this?

But how do we do this? We must see the *future* person rather than the *present* person. We must not see what *is*, but what *could be*. This includes the person in the mirror. Have you been holding yourself back from doing what God wants you to do simply because you are more focused on the *present* you than the *future* you? God focuses on the future us. If we are going to become more like Jesus we must discipline ourselves to see with his eyes. How does Jesus see us? He sees the future. So should we.

This leads to the second way of becoming more like Christ. If we are going to be more like Jesus we not only need to see the world the way he sees the world, but we need to learn to obey his teachings. It can often be overwhelming to think about how we are to follow a God with so many rules. Jesus gave us the secret to living a life that pleases the Father. It is as simple as loving God and loving people! Read on...

Strategy 1 – One Purpose

Mentoring Questions:

- What could be so bad about building a wall just to knock it down again? How do we do this in life? Give examples.
- Why is it so important to have a personal life purpose?
- What does he mean when Preston says Christians should "live in the future"?
- Explain the strategy in a quote using your own words.
- What is one thing you will begin to DO as a result of this strategy? Can I hold you accountable with that?

Make It Count 9

Strategy in a Quote

"In order to fulfill all the laws of God we only need to focus on two: Love God with all your heart, soul, and mind. Love your neighbor as yourself."

12   Strategy 2 – Two Rules

Have you ever played Mao? It is a card game designed to drive you crazy. There are seven rules, but no one can tell you what they are. You just have to figure them out as you go. There are always people who know the rules but they only tell you a rule *after* you have broken it, and only so they can award you a penalty for breaking it! The first time I played this game I almost lost my religion. It made no sense to me why I wasn't allowed to know all the rules up front and it seemed unfair for me to be penalized for breaking a rule I was unaware of. It wasn't until I learned all the rules that I began to love the game. The game gets more interesting the longer you play because at the beginning of each round a new rule is added to the list. After playing fifteen rounds you are fighting to remember all of them and it makes for a really entertaining scene.

I can still remember an evening where I tried teaching my grandmother how to play Mao. She has a terrible memory and only after a few rounds she was already overwhelmed with trying to keep from breaking a rule.

Make It Count

When it was her turn to play a card she would slowly move her card to the discard pile while looking around at each of the players with a look of horror, hoping to read our faces to see if she was breaking a rule by the card she was about to play.

This is a great picture of what life looks like for many Christians today. Many people live in constant fear of breaking a "rule" that they don't enjoy the game of life. The stress of living a good and Godly life sometimes paralyzes people into a life void of excitement and adventure. What a sad way to live.

When Jesus said that he wanted to give us life to the full he never intended for us to live in constant fear of "breaking the rules". Jesus brings freedom, and whom the Son sets free is free indeed! So, how do we live a God-honoring life free of fear and condemnation? We do this by living out two commands of Jesus. Love God with all our heart, soul, and mind. And love our neighbor as ourselves. It's that simple.

Strategy 2 – Two Rules

Love God

Let's quickly explore what it means to love God with everything we are. First, it means we place God as the highest value of our lives. More than our Xbox or sports team, and more than Netflix or any extra-curricular activity we are part of. Loving God with all of our heart, soul, and mind means letting him become our first priority. This sounds easy, but it's actually quite difficult. When was the last time we met with Jesus in prayer? Or read our Bible for something other than a few minutes during church? Why is it that we have a hard time sitting still in a church service for more than thirty minutes, but we have no problem sitting for two hours to watch the latest action movie? It might be a sign that, no matter what we say with our lips, our actions prove we don't really love God with ALL of our heart, soul, and mind.

Now, does loving God with our heart, soul, and mind mean we can't play sports or watch our favorite movies? Of course not. It just means that we should include God in everything we do, and we should set aside significant times just for God and our relationship with him.

Love People

What about loving our neighbor as ourselves? This is also easier said than done. It's easy to love those who love us, but what about our enemies? Does Jesus really expect us to love them as well? Jesus says it this way: *You have heard that it was said, 'Love your neighbor and hate your enemy.' But I tell you, love your enemies and pray for those who persecute you...*[2]

What if Christians began loving their enemies as much as they love themselves? Don't you think that would make a difference? Loving our neighbor as yourself means there are things we do and there are things we don't do. We don't cuss at someone, not because it is bad, but because it is not the most loving thing we could do towards someone. And it does not love our neighbor as ourselves. We don't have premarital sex, not because our parents told us not to, but because it isn't the best

---

[2] Matthew 5:43

way to show love to someone else's future spouse. Plus, giving away a piece of our intimacy is not the most loving thing to do to *our* future spouse.

If we love our neighbor as ourselves we will do certain things we might not have originally done. And we will *not do* certain things we might have done if we were only living for ourselves. We will serve others because we would like to be served. We will speak positively about others because we like it when someone speaks positively of us. We won't harm others because we don't like it when we are harmed. Make sense?

Fulfill the Law

Is it really that simple? All we need to do is love God and love people? Well, look at what Jesus said when asked what was the greatest commandment: *Jesus replied: Love the Lord your God with all your heart and with all your soul and with all your mind.' This is the first and greatest commandment. And the second is like* it: 'Love your neighbor as yourself.' <u>*All the Law and the Prophets hang on these two commandments.*</u>³ *(Emphasis mine)*

When asked what was the most important thing in all the world, Jesus said to love God. But then he added the second most important thing by saying; love your neighbor as yourself. Why did he give more than they asked for? I think it was because of what Jesus said at the end. He knew that if, rather than focusing on all 613 commands the first century Jewish community was trying to live by, we would only focus on two commands then we would actually live up to the other 611.

Imagine playing Mao with 613 different rules to remember! We would break several rules every time we played a card. Imagine living our life in constant fear of breaking the Jewish laws, most of which were actually created by the religious leaders and not by God. Jesus came to bring freedom, not more condemnation. In fact,

---

³ Matthew 22:37-40

Strategy 2 – Two Rules

Paul would say that there is no condemnation for those of us that are found in Christ.

If Jesus intended to give us abundant life he was going to have to refocus us on what matters most. Love God with everything and love people like we love ourselves. All the other "laws" will be fulfilled naturally if we only focus on two. These two commands are like the "decoder ring" for us to know how to please God. This helps to grow us towards maturity and to live the life God called us to.

Now that we have our one purpose and our two rules for life, we need to have a map that shows us where we are and where we need to go. Read on...

Make It Count

Mentoring Questions:

- Can you relate to Preston's grandmother in the opening story? How do we sometimes live like that in our relationship with Jesus?
- How could following only two rules help us fulfill all the other rules God has for us?
- Give examples of how to love God with all our heart, soul, and mind.
- Give examples of how to love our neighbor as ourselves.
- Explain the strategy in a quote using your own words.
- What is one thing you will begin to DO as a result of this strategy? Can I hold you accountable with that?

Strategy in a Quote

"In order to grow closer to God every person will need to meet Jesus, fall in love with Jesus, and serve Jesus. Identify where you are so you will know where you should go."

Strategy 3 – Three Decisions

Have you ever played baseball? Maybe you haven't played before, but you know what it's about because you've been to a game before. Well, baseball is a very simple concept. Two teams are involved and the goal is to score more "runs" than your opposing team. After nine innings the team with the most runs wins the game.

How do you score a run? One of your teammates has to cross home plate. Now, I am about to blow your mind with deep logic: you can't cross home plate without first tagging your foot on third base. Profound, I know! But it gets even better than that. You also can't touch third base without first passing second. #mindblowing

How do you pass second base? Only after touching first base. You already know this stuff. But stay with me for a moment.

What if we could make spiritual maturity as easy to understand as baseball? What if we could see how to move from unbeliever to mature believer like we see how to move from the batter's box to home plate? It would help us see where we are and where we need to be. So, picture a baseball field with the bases in place. Each base represents a step towards spiritual maturity. Let's see if we can apply spiritual growth to a baseball diamond.

Fall in love w/ Jesus

Serve Jesus   Meet Jesus

I often tell people that they fall into one of three categories. They will either need to meet Jesus, fall in love with Jesus, or begin to serve Jesus. I then challenge them to think about where they are on the spiritual formation map. Have they begun a relationship with Jesus? If not, the first step is to get on first base, to start a relationship with him. If they are already on first base and they have a relationship with Jesus then they might need to move to second base, to begin the process of falling in love with him. This is where I invite them to get involved in a small group. If they are falling more and more in love with Jesus then our belief is they will naturally want to begin serving him. This is third base. It's really that simple. But let's look at it a little deeper now.

Spiritual Formation Explored

Batter's Box
The batter's box represents the person who is involved in the game. They are no longer absent from the park and most likely skeptical of Christianity, but they are now open to learning more about this guy named Jesus. They haven't begun a relationship with him yet; they are open to the possibility. Once they decide to move from the batter's box to first base they have officially entered into the family of God.

First Base
First base represents starting a relationship with Jesus. It is called, "Meet Jesus" and it is the first time someone

gives his or her life to the Lord. We have traditionally called this step "salvation". Although this is often viewed as the most important step, it is not the *end* of the journey. It's only the beginning. Sadly, most people who begin a relationship with Jesus may never mature passed their initial salvation experience. They stay on first base. Quick question: If this describes you and you realize that you have never moved passed your salvation experience then what do you think your next step is? Third base? Home plate? Of course not. It is obviously second base, right?

Second Base

For the person who is still on first base, his or her initial salvation experience, the next step is second base. Second base represents going deeper or learning more about Jesus and their faith. It is called, "Fall in love with Jesus" and it is an ongoing thing until the Lord returns or we die. We have traditionally called this step "discipleship". This will mean getting more involved in a small group. Small groups help us stay connected to Jesus through his people and through his word. The

Strategy 3 – Three Decisions

more spiritually intimate relationships we invite into our lives the more likely we will be to move from first to second base. In order to move from first to second there has to be participation from someone other than us. We need others to help progress us from base to base. We must invite others into our lives. This usually looks like sitting in a circle with people who might think differently than we do, and will challenge what we believe and why we believe it. This needs to happen while connecting to Jesus daily through His word and prayer[4]. We will never grow in isolation.

Who are you surrounding yourself with right now? Is it a group of friends that never challenge you? How will you learn to forgive others if there is no one in your life that needs forgiveness? Often, we just hang out with people who think like us, so we have very little conflict. And if someone decides to "buck the system" we just dismiss him or her from our circle. We never have to fight for relationships if all we surround ourselves with are easy relationships. What a small group will do for us

---

[4] See the Connect Four Strategy on page 42

is stretch our worldview and force us to wrestle with difficult questions and relational wisdom. Life doesn't happen in a vacuum. In order to move from first to second we must be actively involved in a small group.

What about those of us who have met Jesus (first base) and have been actively involved in a small group and Bible study (second base) for a number of months or years? What happens when we no longer feel close to Jesus and our faith has become stagnant? We are clearly on second base, but we can't seem to grow anymore. We feel like we need something "deeper" than what we are getting at church and we are no longer "getting" anything out of the services we attend.

Chances are it has little to do with your church leaders. They are probably giving you the same things that once grew you, but now you seem to want more. This is a good thing. It doesn't mean your church is shallow. It actually means they have done a good job maturing you to the point you find yourself now. Send your pastor a thank you card and then recognize that the answer to your issue might be as simple as *you* moving to third base, to begin serving Jesus in a personal ministry.

Third Base

Third base represents giving of our lives for others. It is called, "Serve Jesus" and it is about finding our spiritual gifts and purpose in life so we can begin serving God through building his kingdom. We have traditionally called this step "evangelism, missions, or ministry". But it's really about becoming more like Jesus. Jesus once said, *"The Son did not come to be served, but to serve..."* [5] If we are going to continue growing towards maturity in order to become more like Jesus we must do what he did. We must have the same attitude that Jesus had, *"Who, being in very nature God, did not consider equality with God something to be used to his own advantage; rather, he made himself nothing by taking the very nature of a servant, being made in human likeness."* [6]

---

[5] Matthew 20:28
[6] Philippians 2:6-7

So, are you serving Jesus in some sort of personal ministry? Personal ministry is any ministry you do on a regular basis that you take personal responsibility and ownership of. You don't blame someone else if it struggles to succeed. It is not going on a mission trip once per year or an occasional service project. It is a consistent time of service in which you serve other people. I don't mean you have to be a preacher, musician, or singer. Serving in ministry does not mean being on the stage. It might include that, but ministry is so much more than what we see on the stage. Ministry is simply fulfilling the purpose God has given us personally. Remember our first strategy? Ministry could be defined as nothing more than *helping broken people become whole and whole people become broken for broken people.* Are you broken for the brokenness in the world? If not, pray and ask Jesus to help you see the world through his eyes and not just through your eyes daily. You will begin to see the brokenness that sin causes all around you.

Strategy 3 – Three Decisions

Once you see the brokenness in the world you can ask Jesus what part you play in healing the brokenness. God may want you to focus on mission trips overseas. Or he may ask you to be a missionary to the nursing home down the street. The school hallway is probably the most unreached mission field in America today. Do you want to change the world? Reach your school or workplace for Jesus. God may have gifted you in technology and you could use that gift to serve on the tech team at your church. Some people are very warm and welcoming. Serve on the first impressions, or greeter, team. Some of you might be able to teach, preach, or sing. But some of you can draw, write, and create. Maybe you begin a prayer/encouragement ministry at work for those employees who need to talk to someone safe. You can look at your school or work as a mission field and you are the missionary God has called and sent to be light in that area.

The interesting thing about God is that He created everything we see today. Look around at this wonderfully complex universe He made. Wouldn't you say that God is a pretty creative person? Well, guess what; He created each of us in His image and that means no matter who you are, you have a hint of creativity woven within the very fabric of your being. The math looks like this: *God is creative + God created us in His image = We are creative!*

So we have no excuse for not serving in a personal ministry. Begin to ask God today what type of ministry He would like to see you serve. It will amaze you how much you grow when you simply serve God. God is creative, and He created us in his image. When we exercise our creativity we are actually participating in the divine nature we were created in! Go and serve well.

What about Home Plate?

What is the ultimate "win" in Christianity? It is the same as in baseball, scoring a run by crossing home plate. But what is "home plate" in Christianity? I think it is when we serve God in such a way that it leads to others stepping up to the plate and getting on first base.

Strategy 3 – Three Decisions

Although serving God will help *us* grow towards maturity, the ultimate purpose of third base is to get to home plate. If we say that home plate is helping move others from the batter's box to first base then we have just encouraged the cycle to continue forever. In fact, this cycle has been going on since the creation of the Christian church in Acts chapter two. We are part of a work that God began over two thousand years ago! So, what part are you playing in this cycle? Are you keeping your team from scoring runs because you refuse to run the bases? Or are you encouraging the process from batter's box to home plate with your life and your words? Help broken people become whole by getting more people on first. Help whole people become broken for broken people by helping more people round the bases and cross home plate.

Christianity is a life-long *process*, not a one-time *decision*. God created this process. How does God expect to accomplish this process? He has set up two places where this process is to be fleshed out. Read on...

Make It Count

Mentoring Questions:

- Explain in your own words what each base on the baseball diamond represents. Describe what the person looks like at each base of the spiritual formation map.
- Using the baseball diamond as a spiritual formation map of where we are in our spiritual journey, where are you on that map?
- What would your next step be in growing in your relationship with Jesus?
- Give examples of how we can apply what Preston means when he says "God is creative + God created us in His image = We are creative!"
- According to Preston, what is the "ultimate win" for the Christian?
- What are some ways we can accomplish the "win"?
- What is one thing you will begin to DO as a result of this strategy? Can I hold you accountable with that?

Strategy in a Quote

"God established two institutions where spiritual growth could happen - the family and the church. We need to prioritize, participate with, strengthen, honor, and protect both."

Strategy 4 – Two Priorities

I have seven large pecan trees in my yard. They shed dead branches all the time. What if I walked outside one day and began screaming at the dead branches to produce pecans? Would they be able to do so? No. Why? Because they are no longer connected to the source in order to receive the proper nutrients to produce pecans. On the flip side, what if I went outside and demanded the healthy trees to stop producing pecans? Would they be able to obey? No!

Why not? The reason is because the only option for a branch that is connected to a healthy tree is to produce the fruit of that tree.

Jesus once told his disciples that in order for them to produce fruit they would need to remain in him. In other words, Jesus needed them to connect with him and to stay connected to him, like a branch is connected to a tree trunk. The roots absorb the nutrients from the ground and deliver it to the trunk. The trunk stores and distributes those nutrients to the branches. The branches then produce fruit. It's that simple.

In order for us to actually live a life that pleases God we need to stay connected to Jesus. But how do we do this? Before we answer this question we need to have a better understanding of God's plan for second base (discipleship).

Did you know that there are only two things God established to accomplish discipleship? It's true! God knew that for discipleship to happen it would need to happen within the context of relationships. The first thing God established was the home and the second was the church.

The Home

The Home - God's first institution. *Then God said, 'Let us make man in our image, in our likeness...Then God made mankind in his own image, in the image of God he created them; male and female he created them.*[7] God told Adam and Eve to *be fruitful and multiply and to fill the earth and subdue it; Rule over the fish in the sea*

---

[7] Genesis 1:26

and the birds in the sky and over every living creature that moves on the ground.[8]

For this reason a man will leave his father and mother and be united to his wife and the two will become one flesh.[9] So God set up, from the beginning, the family unit to be his method of service and discipleship to the world. A friend of mine, Jason Richards, recently brought to my attention that after the flood waters subsided and Noah got off the boat with all the animals we see something very interesting written in the text. The English Standard Version translates Genesis 8:18-19 like this:

> *"So Noah went out, and his sons and his wife and his sons' wives with him. Every beast, every creeping thing, and every bird, everything that moves on the earth, went out by <u>families</u> from the ark."* *(Emphasis mine)*

---

[8] Genesis 1:28
[9] Genesis 2:24

Jason pointed out that when God was setting up "Earth 2.0" he once again started with the family.

Home is a place where life happens more freely. Home is where we can be ourselves all the time. Did you realize that parents have about 3,000 hours per year with their children? Compare this to the 40-50 hours per year the church has with the average student. Which institution do you think has the greatest potential for influence? For better or for worse, the home has so much more potential for influence. So, let's find ways to bring the spiritual conversation we begin at church home with us.

Hopefully, you have an open relationship and an open line of communication with your family. This is an important component to connecting with Jesus at home. Bible study is so much better with the family in the living room. Scripture is more potent when read in the bedroom. Spiritual conversations are so much deeper in the realm of a healthy relationship with family members. Start viewing the home as the first, and best, life-giving place.

The Church

The Church - God's second institution. Jesus mentions the impact the church would soon have on the world when He said, *"...I will build my church, and the gates of Hades will not overcome it."* [10] My pastor once preached a message on this passage. He said the interesting truth about this passage is that gates in bible times were always used to keep people out. So when Jesus said the gates of Hades would not overcome, He was implying something that we miss too often. When we read this passage, we tend to think that Hades is on the offense and we are on the defense. But if this were true, then Jesus would have said, "the gates of *Heaven* would not overcome" since gates were meant to keep something or someone *out*. In other words, if Hades were on the offense, then we would be on the defense.

Since we know that gates were designed to keep people out, when Jesus says that Hades will not overcome, we know He is expecting the church not to be on defense,

---

[10] Matthew 16:18

but offense! Too many churches are living in a state of defense. Jesus calls us to storm the gates of Hell because the gates will not overcome the power of the cross!

Fifty days after Jesus was raised from the dead we see Him pour out the Holy Spirit on the believers at Pentecost. At this moment He establishes His church. The church is the second institution He commissions to bring discipleship to the world. The church is not a building. The church is a movement of God. It is a collection of Jesus-followers that work together to establish the kingdom of God on Earth as it is in Heaven. Jesus is the king. His people are His body, the church.

The church is a place where we connect with Jesus through His people. This is a place where we can learn how to forgive others, confess our struggles, collaborate together, worship, and serve. The church is the institution God established to fulfill His great commission to reach the world with the good news of Jesus.

Strategy 4 – Two Priorities

So, we have established that in order to live a life pleasing to God we must stay connected to Jesus. We have briefly looked at the two institutions God has established for discipleship (fall in love with Jesus). How do these two places help us stay connected to Jesus?

Connect Four

Connect Four is an attempt to help us connect with Jesus at home and at church on a regular basis throughout the year. The challenges in the Connect Four strategy are broken down into daily, weekly, monthly, and yearly. Here they are:

Connect with Jesus at home through His word daily.
- This means that we should strive to read His word daily. This really isn't that hard to do. If we want to grow towards maturity we must prioritize our time in scripture. Just give God one episode of your favorite show once per day a week and, instead of watching it, have a quiet time or listen to a chapter of the Bible in your Bible app.

Connect with Jesus at church through His people weekly.

- This is extremely doable. Think about it. We should prioritize our church attendance anyway. So if we truly want to move towards maturity we should at least attend church once per week. That would equal four days per month. Maybe you can't make every Sunday, but chances are your church has other days of the week than just Sunday for you to find a worship service and small group. Make spending time with other Christians a higher priority than sports or other things. It will be worth it in the end.

Connect with a mentor/accountability partner monthly.

- Few things are more important than accountable relationships with people you can trust. People who love you and are willing to speak hard truths into your life are people worth hanging out with. Proverbs 27:6 says, "The wounds of a friend can be trusted, but the kisses of an enemy are many." The question you need to ask is this: do I want a true friend or a bunch of enemies?

Strategy 4 – Two Priorities

Most people only want to have "friends" that tell them how awesome they are. But according to this verse, a true friend is willing to tell you what you *need* to hear, even if it isn't what you *want* to hear. Accountability conversations look like this:

<u>True Friend</u> - "Do you want me to be your friend or your enemy?"
<u>You</u> - "I don't want you to be my enemy! I want you to be my friend."
<u>True Friend</u> - "Then what I am about to say might hurt you, but know who it is coming from. I am your friend…"

Then the accountability partner will tell the person they are talking to what they observe in his or her life that needs adjusting. Make sense? Use the *C4* journal to help you with accountable relationships. There is a section for accountability relationships that explains what these relationships should look like and what to do when you meet together. The goal is to meet together monthly.

Connect with Jesus through extracurricular events yearly.

- This is where it gets fun. Choose a Christian concert or conference to attend. Go with your small group. Attend camp or a mission trip. When I say "extracurricular event" all I mean is an event that is not part of your churches weekly schedule. Your church probably offers fun events throughout the year. Let these be one of your extracurricular events. The reason I encourage this is so you don't get stagnant and routine in your faith. We all need times when we can get a "shot in the arm" of spirituality. This is why prioritizing extracurricular events throughout the year is so important.

Connect four people to Jesus along the way.

- We will never grow to our full potential until we help others connect with Jesus. This might look like inviting one of your friends to an event designed to help them meet Jesus. It might mean you take one of these friends to an extracurricular event with your small group. It really could be as simple as sitting at the lunch table sharing the verse of the day from your Bible app. However you choose to connect your friends to Jesus you need to be in constant prayer for them. Lee Strobel often says, "Before we talk to our friends about God we need to talk to God about our friends."

If you would like more help with the Connect Four strategy you can pick up one of our *C4* journals that is designed to be a journal companion for your quiet time guides as you connect with God's word daily. It guides you through listening to the entire New Testament in one year by only playing a little more than one chapter per day, four days per week through your Bible app. It also has a place for you to take sermon notes while you are connecting with God's people at church weekly. It even has a section for your extracurricular events as well as four blanks on the bottom of each week's page so you can write down the four names of friends you are praying will connect with Jesus throughout the year. This journal is just a simple tool to help put into practice the Connect Four strategy.

No matter how you choose to connect with Jesus, I encourage you to highly prioritize connecting with Jesus at home and at church on a regular and consistent basis. Remember what Jesus said, *"If you remain in me and I in you, you will bear much fruit; apart from me you can do nothing."* [11]

---

[11] John 15:5

Strategy 4 – Two Priorities

Mentoring Questions:

- What are the two institutions God established where spiritual growth could happen?
- Why is it so important to have a proper love and respect for these institutions?
- Give examples of ways people often mistreat these two institutions.
- Give examples of ways we can prioritize, participate with, strengthen, honor, and protect both.
- Explain the Connect Four strategy.
- How are you doing with connecting to Jesus in that way?
- What is one thing you will begin to DO as a result of this strategy? Can I hold you accountable with that?

Make It Count

Strategy in a Quote

"If life is going to work as it was originally intended we must try to keep the main thing the main thing. Jesus is the main thing! Everything we do is for the ultimate purpose of bringing glory to Him."

Strategy 5 – One Person

To conclude this book I feel like we should examine the prophet Jonah. Hold on! Don't skip this strategy simply because you have already read the story of Jonah or watched the movie. This is the most important strategy of the entire book. So, please read on...

Exploring Jonah

The story of Jonah begins with the word of the Lord coming to Jonah. God tells Jonah to go to Nineveh and preach against it, because its wickedness has come up before the Lord. But Jonah runs from the Lord. Right off the bat, Jonah hears from God and disobeys. Spoiler alert: we find out in the final chapter why Jonah runs from the Lord. It is NOT because he is afraid of the Ninevites, but because he hates them. Nineveh was the capital city of Assyria. Assyria was a ruthless enemy of Israel. Before Rome perfected crucifixion, Assyria perfected the art of skinning people alive. They were evil and harsh. So yes, Jonah might have been a bit scared to preach against Nineveh. However, fear was not his main motive for disobeying God. He hated the Assyrians and wanted them to perish. So we see him run from the Lord and head to Tarshish in the opposite direction. It would seem like Jonah thought he could actually remove himself from the Lord's presence. This is the first clue that Jonah had a vision problem. He had a *small* view of God. Also, prophets were God's instruments to speak God's message to the people on God's behalf. Jonah's main job as a prophet was to hear from God and speak what he heard. He was to be God's mouthpiece to the world. Jonah, however, thought he had the right to choose which messages he would preach and which messages he would repress. So, Jonah had a *small* view of God and a *big* view of himself.

You know the story. Jonah runs away from the mission. God sends a storm. The sailors cast lots to see who is the cause of the storm. Jonah confesses and is thrown overboard. The storm stops. A great fish swallows up Jonah and he smells really bad for at least three days! I would think this might change Jonah's view of the call just a bit. And it does,

Jonah's view of God becomes bigger and his view of himself becomes smaller. He cries out to God, and God has the great fish spit Jonah up on the shore. The word of the Lord comes to Jonah a second time--and Jonah obeys. This is encouraging for you and for me. As the Veggietales movie about Jonah so accurately communicates in a song, God is a God of second chances. Jonah obeys and goes to Nineveh to preach against it, and the people hear the message and repent. From the top down, Nineveh repents of their ways and gets right with God. In a massive, citywide revival, the whole city is saved. Jonah must be so excited...right? Wrong. *"But to Jonah this seemed very wrong, and he became angry. He prayed to the Lord, 'Isn't this what I said, Lord, when I was still at home? That is why I tried to forestall by fleeing to Tarshish. I knew that you were a gracious and compassionate God, slow to anger and abounding in love, a God who relents from sending calamity. Now, Lord, take away my life, for it is better for me to die than to live.' But the Lord replied, "Is it right for you to be angry?'"*[12]

---

[12] Jonah 4:1-4

Jonah doesn't even answer God's question. Instead, he leaves the city and sits on a hill; watching and hoping God might still destroy the very people Jonah had just witnessed come to Him. Jonah gets hot and tired and makes a shelter for himself. He is trying to get a good seat to watch the destruction. Once again, Jonah has a small view of God and a big view of Jonah. He has a distorted view of the call.

Jonah felt it unjust that God would offer the Ninevites forgiveness. He even screams at God and pretty much says, "I knew you were a good God. That's why I didn't want to go to Nineveh. I knew that if they would turn to you then you would forgive them. I hated them so much I wanted to withhold information from them so that they would die and go to Hell. God, you ruined my plan!" In a real sense, Jonah was trying to be God. He was trying to be the one to choose who received grace and who didn't. All the while God was showing *him* grace after grace. It reminds me of the parable of the "unmerciful servant" in Matthew 18:21-35.

God is gracious to Jonah and gives him a leafy plant to give him relief from the sun, and Jonah is happy. But the next day God sends a worm to eat the plant and make it wither. Jonah complains again that he'd rather die than live. God then questions him by saying, "Is it right for you to be angry about this plant?" Notice how God asks the same question in a different context. "Is it right for you to be angry..." (4:4, 4:9) Jonah shows us once again his distorted view of the God of the universe when he says, "It is! I am so angry I wish I were dead." #whatababy

Then God concludes with Jonah 4:10-11: "You have been concerned about this plant, though you did not tend it or make it grow. It sprang up overnight and died overnight. And should I not have concern for the great city of Nineveh, in which there are more than a hundred and twenty thousand people who cannot tell their right hand from their left--and also many animals?"

And that is the conclusion of the book. What a lousy ending! It's almost as if the writer wanted to leave the reader with this uncomfortable interlude between what *was* and what *should be*. God speaks. Jonah disobeys. God disciplines. Jonah obeys. God blesses. Jonah gets mad. God speaks again. The end. Now what? Where is the prophetic message from God to his people? Where is the resolution of the story? Where is the closure?

Understanding Jonah

Here is the secret to understanding the message of this book: the story of Jonah *IS* the message of God to His people. The people of God had a distorted view of the call of God on their lives. They believed they were more important than all other nations simply because God had chosen them to be His people. But if you will remember, God chose them for a specific purpose. It wasn't that God loved Israel more than any other nation. Clearly God cared about the people of Nineveh too. Israel was NOT called by God to sit in the blessings of being "God's people" without doing anything for the rest of the world. God expected Israel to be His light to a lost world in order to bring all nations back to Him.

There are many verses that inform us of the purposes of Israel. They were *blessed* to be a *blessing*. They were called to be the light to the nations, so the nations would know who the only true God was. God *called* them, not to salvation but to a purpose. The purpose was to proclaim God to the nations and to make Him famous, to make broken people whole. And, just like Jonah in the story, Israel was not fulfilling their God-given call. They had a distorted view of the call and of the One doing the calling. Jonah was a representative of Israel. So, the story of Jonah *IS* the story of Israel. When God spoke to Jonah He was actually speaking to Israel.

When the Lord replied, "Is it right for you to be angry?" He was actually saying, "Israel, who are you to be angry about me blessing Nineveh? That is what YOU were *called* to do. I have given you grace after grace, and how do you respond? Like a spoiled brat throwing a temper tantrum." Jesus later would use the parable of the "unmerciful servant" to illustrate a similar point. And that's the story of Jonah.

Make It Count

Applying Jonah

Just like Jonah, we sometimes can lose our focus. We can be more focused on our desires and interests. We can set ourselves up as king, and lose a proper view of the call.

We must be careful not to lose focus of the kingdom work in the world. It's bigger than your life or my life. Even though we are part of the kingdom work, we're a small part. When we only focus on our little world, we begin to believe that this is all that matters. And if this is all that matters, then we are somebody special. Ultimately the world revolves around our lives and our perspectives.

When this shift of perspective happens, we lose focus of the kingdom work and we don't fully see the kingdom. If we develop a faulty view of the kingdom, we can't see who the real King is. And then we become the king in our Kingdom--and Jesus is just our servant.

Strategy 5 – One Person

If life is going to work as it was originally intended we must try to keep the main thing the main thing. Jesus is the main thing. Everything we do is for the ultimate purpose of bringing glory to Him. Below is an excerpt from a sermon Dr. Richard Ross preached on the supremacy of Christ. He has given me permission to share this with you now. This is the Savior we serve:

The words you are about to read have their origin in the divine realm. God's word is powerful and effective. So, read carefully and, if possible, read it out loud in order to preach it to yourself. See if your view of Jesus doesn't change after this is over.

In the beginning was the word. And the word was with God and the word was God. He is the image of the invisible God. By Him all things were created, both in Heaven and on Earth, visible and invisible. Whether thrones or dominions or rulers or authorities all things have been created through Him and for Him. He is before all things and in Him all things hold together.

Make It Count

Then God said, "Let us make man in our image whom I have created for my glory." But she took the fruit and she ate. And she gave some to her husband who was with her and Adam ate. Through one man sin entered into the world and death through sin. And so death spread to all men for all have sinned. And men began to multiple on the face of the land. All of us like sheep have gone astray. Each of us has turned to his own way. For all have sinned and fall short of the glory of God. And the wages of sin is death.

The Lord will judge his people. It is a terrifying thing to fall into the hands of the living God. But God so loved the world that He gave His only son that whoever believes in Him would not perish but have eternal life. Therefore, the Lord Himself will give you a sign. Behold! A virgin will be with child and she will call His name Emmanuel. Christ emptied Himself taking the form of a bondservant being made in the likeness of men. And Mary gave birth to her firstborn son and the Word became flesh and made His dwelling among us.

Strategy 5 – One Person

And the child grew in wisdom and stature and the grace of God was upon him. Now, from this time Jesus began to preach "Repent! For the kingdom of heaven is near!" Now after six days Jesus took with him Peter, James, and John and He led them up a high mountain. There, He was transfigured before them. His face shone like the sun and His clothes became as white as the light. A bright cloud enveloped them and a voice from the cloud said, "This is my Son, whom I love. Listen to Him."

Now the disciples came to Him privately saying, "Tell us. What will be the sign of your coming and of the end of the age?" Jesus said to them, "This gospel of the kingdom shall be preached to the whole world as a testimony to all the nations and then the end will come. And they will see the Son of Man coming on the clouds in the sky with power and great glory.

Then men seized Jesus and arrested Him and took Him to Caiaphas the High Priest. The High Priest said to Him, "I charge you under oath by the living God. Tell us if you're the Christ, the Son of God." "Yes! It is as you say. And in the future you will see the Son of Man sitting at the right hand of the mighty one and coming on the clouds of Heaven. Then the High Priest tore his clothes and he said, "He has spoken blasphemy! We don't need any more witnesses! What do you think?" And they answered, "He is worthy of death!" And when they had come to the place, which is called the skull, there they crucified Him. The Lord was pleased to crush Him. Smitten of God. He laid on Him the iniquity of us all. He Himself bore our sins in His body on the cross so that we might die to sin and live to righteousness.

Christ died for sins to bring us to God. Joseph took the body and wrapped it in a clean linen cloth and laid it in his own new tomb. As it began to dawn on the first day of the week Mary Magdalene and the other Mary came to look at the grave. And behold! An angel of the Lord descended from Heaven and came and rolled away the stone. The angel said to the women, "Do not be afraid, for I know that you are looking for Jesus who was crucified. HE IS NOT HERE. HE HAS RISEN!

Now, to the apostles Jesus presented Himself alive after His suffering, appearing to them over a period of forty days. And He led them out as far as Bethany and He lifted up His hands and He blessed them. "You will receive power when the Holy Spirit comes upon you and you shall be my witnesses both in Jerusalem and in all Judea and Samaria and even to the remotest parts of the earth.

And after He had said these things He was lifted up while they were looking on. And a cloud received Him out of their sight. He was clothed in a robe reaching to His feet and girded across His chest was a golden sash. His head and His hair were white like wool, like snow. And His eyes were like flames of fire. And God said, "Sit at my right hand until I make your enemies a footstool for your feet. God seated Him at His right hand in the Heavenly places far above all rule and authority and power and dominion.

Now, when the day of Pentecost had come and they were all together in one place and suddenly there came from heaven a sound like a violent rushing wind and it filled the whole house where they were sitting. Peter raised his voice and declared to them, "This Jesus God raised up again, which we are all witnesses. Therefore, having been exalted to the right hand of God and having received from the Father the promise of the Holy Spirit He has poured forth this, which you both see and hear. Therefore, let all the house of Israel know for certain that God has made Him both Lord and Christ. This Jesus that you crucified! Now when they heard this they were cut to the heart and they said, "What shall we do to be saved?" Peter said, "Repent, each of you and be baptized in the name of Jesus Christ for the forgiveness of your sins and you will receive the Holy Spirit."

The grace of God has appeared bringing salvation to all men instructing us to deny ungodliness and worldly desires and to live righteously and Godly in this present age, looking for the appearing of the glory of our great God and Savior, Jesus Christ. The Lord, Himself, will descend from Heaven with a shout, with the voice of the archangel and with the trumpet of God. And the dead in Christ will rise first. Then, we who are alive and remain will be caught up together with them to meet the Lord in the air. And when the Son of Man comes in His glory and all of His angels with Him then He will sit on His glorious throne. All the nations will be gathered before Him and He will separate them, one from another. He will say to those on His left, "Depart from me accursed ones, into the eternal fire which has been prepared for the Devil and his angels." Then the king will say to those on His right, "Come, you who are blessed by my Father. Inherit the kingdom prepared for you from the foundation of the world."

And there was a multitude no one could count from every nation, tribe, people, and language singing, "To Him who sits on the throne and to the Lamb be PRAISE and HONOR and GLORY and POWER forever and ever!"

Jesus said, "I am the way and the truth and the life. No one comes to the Father except through me. Behold! I am coming soon. I am the Alpha and the Omega, the first and the last, the beginning and the end."

Conclusion

The next time we are tempted to make life about us, we need to reread this section. Let it remind us exactly how majestic King Jesus really is. He is supreme over everything we could ever possess. He is glorious and precious. He is not some genie in a bottle that sits waiting to fulfill our requests. He doesn't work for us. He is sitting on the throne of the Universe and we must recognize the extreme privilege it is to serve on HIS team. Yes, He is gracious. Yes, we can approach the throne with confidence. But this does not mean that we take His supremacy lightly. And God help us when we attempt, consciously or unconsciously, to make Christianity more about *US* and less about *JESUS*. He will not share His glory with anyone. We must be careful to submit to His leadership at all times.

Maybe today you realize for the first time that you have been treating Jesus in an inappropriate way, and today you need to stop. Spend a moment now asking Him to forgive you and to help you to have a more clear view of Him from now on. 1 John 1:9 says, "If you confess your sins, He is faithful and just to forgive you of your sins and cleanse you from all unrighteousness." Thank Him for His forgiveness today.

Or maybe this new view of King Jesus is helping you to finally believe He is big enough to take care of your needs. Spend a moment now telling Him you will do what He asks you to do even if you don't see how He will provide. Tell Him you are willing to step out of the boat and trust Him with your life. As it says in Matthew 6:33, "Seek first His kingdom and His righteousness, and all these things will be added unto you."

Now that we know who the real Jesus is and have a proper view of the call and the Caller, let's pray in response to what we have just seen and heard. Only Jesus can truly bless our lives. The strategies in this book are worthless without Him. Nothing trumps the favor of God on our life. So, I challenge you to close this book, kneel at this time, and pray to King Jesus. Sit in His presence for a while. Then, get up and walk in victory!

Make It Count

Mentoring Questions:

- Explain the story of Jonah in your own words.
- What was Jonah's biggest mistake?
- How do we sometimes make that same mistake?
- Give examples of how we sometimes treat Jesus in inappropriate ways.
- What must we do to stop treating Jesus in those ways?
- How are you doing lately with submitting to Jesus as king?
- What is one area of your life that you have not given Jesus ownership?
- What is one thing you will begin to DO as a result of this strategy? Can I hold you accountable with that?

CONCLUSION

Make It Count

To conclude this book I'd like to share with you a story I heard many years ago that has helped me continue to move towards maturity.

"You Choose"

There once was an old man who often fed pigeons on a park bench. Two young boys often walked through the park and would taunt him, asking him many riddles. The boys would think long and hard to find the perfect riddle that the man wouldn't be able to solve, but they were never able to outwit this wise old man.

One day the oldest boy came across a wounded bird lying on the ground. He grabbed the bird and ran to the other boy excited to share his master plan. The plan was simple. Go to the old man with the bird behind his back. Tell the old man that he has a bird behind his back. Ask the man if the bird is dead or alive. If the old man says the bird is dead then the boys will show him that the bird is alive. But if the man says the bird is alive then the boy holding it will squeeze the bird to death and show the old man that it was indeed dead. They thought they had finally come up with the ultimate trick question that would finally stump this wise old man!

They came to the man on the same park bench he always sat. They looked at him and said, "Old man, I have a bird behind my back. Is the bird dead or alive?" The man sat in silence as he fed the pigeons. "I said…I have a bird behind my back. Is it dead or is it alive?" asked the boy again. There was still no response from the man. "OLD MAN! I have a bird behind my back. Is the bird dead or is it alive?" The boy raised his voice in an attempt to force a response. At this, the old man stood and looked in the direction of the two boys. The man spoke in his slow, deep voice, "The answer to your question is lying in the palm of your hand. YOU CHOOSE!" He sat back down and continued to feed the pigeons as the two boys slowly walked away.

The point of this story is that we all have a choice to make. We can read a book like this and walk away with only head knowledge. Or we can read these strategies and take them to heart, actually applying them to our lives. The choice is ultimately yours. You choose if you will apply these strategies to your life, or if you will walk away unchanged.

When these strategies are lived out in your life they will transform you into the image of Jesus and your life will truly count. When these strategies are tossed aside and forgotten then you will never change. The choice is yours. What will you do?

Will you make your life count?
(Check YES or NO)

YES
☐

NO
☐

Made in the USA
Columbia, SC
27 January 2022